Canada Votes

How we elect our government

Written by **Linda Granfield**

Illustrations by **Craig Terlson**

Kids Can Press

First revised edition, 1992
Second revised edition, 1994
Third revised edition, 1997
Fourth revised edition, 2000
Fifth revised edition, 2001

Kids Can Press Ltd.
29 Birch Avenue
Toronto, Ontario, Canada
M4V 1E2

Kids Can Press acknowledges the financial support of the
Ontario Arts Council, the Canada Council for the Arts and
the Government of Canada, through the BPIDP, for our
publishing activity.

Edited by Valerie Wyatt
Designed by Michael Solomon
Printed and bound in Canada

CDN 01   0 9 8 7 6 5 4 3 2 1

Canadian Cataloguing in Publication Data

Granfield, Linda
    Canada votes : how we elect our government

5th rev. ed.
Includes index.
ISBN 1-55337-009-0

1. Elections — Canada — Juvenile literature.
2. Voting — Canada — Juvenile literature.
I. Terlson, Craig.   II. Title.

JL193.G73 2001   j324.971   C00-931534-9

Kids Can Press is a Nelvana company

Acknowledgements

An information book represents only a smidgen of the materials collected and one quickly learns to ferret out the best sources to make the job as painless and pleasurable as possible. Digging for information happily brings choice tidbits, but it also gives birth to welcome, albeit short-lived, encounters with people enthusiastic about what they do. My thanks go to the following people for sharing their spirit and information with me: first, my editor Val Wyatt and the rest of the Kids Can family for offering me yet another opportunity to write and then yellow-slipping me to a proper finished product; to Michael Solomon for a wonderful design and Craig Terlson for his humorous illustrations.

My gratitude is extended as well to Herschell Sax, John Enright, Christine Jackson and Jacques Mackay at Elections Canada for bringing their expertise and updated information to this project; to the staff of the Baldwin Room, Metropolitan Toronto Public Library; the staffs of Elections Ontario, the Canadian National Institute for the Blind, and the National Film Board of Canada; Peter Brennan, Don Cameron, Brian Potvin and Julie Dunbar of the Hansard Reporting Service; John D. Leach of the Clerk's Department at Etobicoke City Hall, Etobicoke, Ontario; and Peter St. Pierre of the Liquor Control Board of Ontario, who made the extra efforts needed to learn about that demon rum and the law.

Finally, hugs to Devon and Brian Smiley, who supported this candidate throughout the election-book campaign. Undoubtedly, they will remember to call in some of my campaign promises!

For Cal
with memories of New York
pizza and Ottawa politics

Table of Contents

The Right to Vote — Your Right to Vote

⊗ EVERY COUPLE OF YEARS, SIGNS SEEM TO SPROUT ON the lawns of your neighbourhood. Sure, you think, another election — but have you thought about why we have elections? Maybe they're just a way to create more jobs? Maybe they're a waste of time and money? Maybe you don't have to think about them until you're an adult?

Not so.

In a democracy like Canada's, it is the right and privilege of the people to elect the men and women who will govern them. Your right to vote is protected by the Constitution — no one can deny you the right to vote because of your race, religious beliefs or sex. Not everyone on Earth has this protected right. In some countries people are never asked to choose a new government; they are forced to accept whatever group seizes power. They can't cast their votes and throw a person out of office; they must find other ways, such as violence, to make their needs and wishes known.

Canada's system of government is based on the British model of *responsible government*. This means that the decisions and acts of the prime minister and his Cabinet (which the prime minister selects) must be approved by a vote in the House and the Senate. Members of Parliament are answerable (or "responsible") to the people of Canada.

Voters must also be responsible. You may have to wait until you are 18 to vote in a federal election, but you are voting in your home or in the classroom more often than you think. Learning about elections and voting makes each one of us a powerful part of our communities and our country.

Get ready to make your mark!

Winds of change

The multiple-party system with regular elections is the method we use to elect a new government in Canada, but it's not the only way a country can get new leadership.

Some countries, such as Cuba, have a one-party system. This means that all the candidates belong to the same party. Voters can choose between candidates, but there is no choice of parties as there is in Canada.

Many countries, including Russia and its neighbours, once had one-party systems. Then, in the early 1990s, the people in these countries demanded and won multi-party systems.

The people of Communist China were not successful in their quest for a democratically elected government. Despite public demonstrations, China remains a one-party nation where voters have little choice. But political situations can change quickly, and it's plain to see that the voters of the world generate a great deal of power. Their voice is impossible to ignore for long.

South Africa is a good example. Up until recently, only white people were allowed to vote. After years of demonstrations and discussions, black and coloured South Africans finally were given the right to vote in 1994. With the 1994 election, South Africa became truly democratic.

Who Can Vote?

ONCE YOU'VE TURNED 18, YOU'LL BE ELIGIBLE TO vote. What happens in the Canadian government is then up to you — and 20 million other voters.

In the past, some Canadians were denied the right to vote because of their ethnic origin, gender or religion. People who didn't own property couldn't vote either. Today, you can vote if you are a Canadian citizen, at least 18 years old and your name appears on the register of electors drawn up for each election. Your ethnic background, gender and religion have nothing to do with your right to vote.

You can even vote if you are a prisoner serving fewer than two years in a correctional institution. What about the judge who sentences the prisoner? For a time, federally appointed judges couldn't vote. They couldn't be involved in politics in any way. In 1988 the judges went to court and won the right to vote.

Getting on the register of electors is an important first step towards voting. But nothing — including the register — is perfect. Sometimes under-age teens find their names on the register by mistake. In 1988, a dog's name was found on a list of voters in a Toronto election. No, it did not vote.

Hang in there! After your eighteenth birthday you'll have won the right to vote — it's guaranteed by law.

So Who Actually Votes?

People sometimes complain that the government doesn't give them a chance to change what they don't like. But not all people who have the right to vote use that right. What a waste!

- In national (federal) elections, one-quarter of the voters don't vote. (In a U.S. presidential election almost half the voters — 45 percent — never vote.)
- In most provincial elections, even fewer voters vote. (Quebec is the exception; more voters cast ballots in provincial elections than in federal elections.)
- In municipal (city or town) elections, the voter turnout is the lowest of all.

And size isn't everything at election time:

- Smaller provinces such as Prince Edward Island and New Brunswick often have the highest voter turnout.
- Meanwhile, a large province such as Alberta can have the lowest voter turnout in both federal and provincial elections.

Votes...and alphabet soup

This book concentrates on the federal elections in Canada: but as a newly listed voter, you have lots of other people to vote in (or out) of office, too.

• On the municipal (city or town) level of government, you vote for a mayor, councillors, school trustees and local representatives. In some towns people once voted for fence viewers (the person who settled fence disputes between neighbours) and dog-catchers.

• In provincial elections, you elect members of the Provincial Parliament (MPPs). In Quebec, the members of the Provincial Parliament, called the National Assembly, are called MNAs, and in Newfoundland, members of the House Assembly are known as MHAs. And let's add just one more spoonful of letters to this alphabet soup. The members of some other provincial legislatures are MLAs, or members of the Legislative Assembly.

More Chances to Vote

INITIAL BALLOT BEFORE FOLDING
PARAFER BULLETIN DE VOTE
AVANT DE PLIER

1 Forest / forêt

2 Gorge / gorge

3 Mountain / montagne

4 Prairie / prairie

5 Seashore / b

INITIAL BALLOT BEFORE FOLDING
PARAFER BULLETIN DE VOTE
AVANT DE PLIER

1 Baseball / base-ball

2 Basketball / basket-ball

3 Football / football

4 Hockey / hockey

As you've seen, there are plenty of opportunities to get out and vote. By-elections and referendums provide two more chances to have your say.

A *by-election* is a special election held between elections in order to fill vacant seats in a provincial or federal legislature. Sometimes a member dies, retires or becomes ill and is unable to fulfil his or her duties. The voters in the riding still need a spokesperson in Parliament, so a by-election is held to fill the seat.

A *referendum* is a different kind of vote. It takes place when a very important public question must be decided. Most decisions are made by our elected representatives: referendum issues are decided directly by the people. Sometimes the referendum issue is added to the ballot during an election. Other times, a referendum means a separate visit to the polls.

For example, in a city election, the voters in an area where liquor is not sold might vote on the referendum issue of whether to allow the sale of alcoholic beverages. Federal referendums, called plebiscites, are rare. The last one, in 1992, was on constitutional changes.

Who's the Boss?

Who's Minding the Store?

The returning officers are the key officials in each electoral district. They are appointed by the federal Cabinet. The returning officers co-ordinate the election process in their electoral district. They also set up advance polls, receive candidates' nomination papers and have the register of electors and ballots printed.

SUPPOSE YOU HEARD THAT YOUR FAVOURITE POP star was going to tour in your area. You'd rush to get more information and, better yet, tickets for great seats. Imagine your frustration if you couldn't find out who was in charge of the tour; if everyone you phoned passed you along to another office. The date for the concert was set, yet you couldn't get a ticket. If only someone knew what was going on!

Holding an election is a bit like staging a rock concert. It's a big event that requires lots of organization. Someone has to be in charge. During a federal election, that someone is the chief electoral officer (CEO). It's his or her job to oversee every detail.

The moment an election is called, the CEO contacts all the returning officers around the country so they can start working on the election. Later, formal notification, called writs of election, is sent out. The CEO and his or her co-workers have a little over a month from the announcement of a federal election to election day. That's

Elections Canada

All federal elections in Canada are organized and run by an agency of Parliament called Elections Canada. This agency is *non-partisan*; that means it is not influenced by and doesn't support any one political party. Elections Canada protects the rights of all Canadian voters to participate freely in each federal election. To keep Canadian voters informed, Elections Canada staff members help to prepare 600 tonnes of printed material. They send out half a million cheques to pay rentals, salaries and other expenses.

Elections Canada moves with the times. Electronic data processing was used for the first time during the 1988 election. Computers generated up-to-date electoral information quickly and efficiently. Electronic mail saved time and money.

Elections Canada oversees the voting process. For more information, check out their web site (http://www.elections.ca).

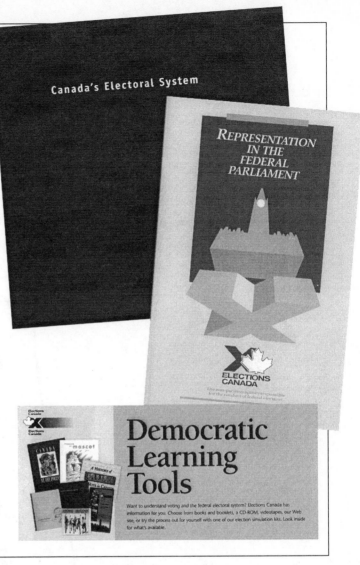

Canada's Electoral System

REPRESENTATION IN THE FEDERAL PARLIAMENT

ELECTIONS CANADA

Democratic Learning Tools

Want to understand voting and the federal electoral system? Elections Canada has information for you. Choose from books and booklets, a CD-ROM, videotapes, our Web site, or try the process out for yourself with one of our election simulation kits. Look inside for what's available.

Fourteen million and one, fourteen million and two...

Holding an election in Canada is a big job. Just imagine what it would be like in India, where there are 250 million voters. More than *15 million* ballot boxes are needed for a general election!

not very long to train thousands of poll officers, review the register of electors and take care of millions of voters, voting places and ballots.

Believe it or not, the CEO co-ordinates the entire election — but he can't vote himself! He must remain impartial.

The CEO's job isn't over on election day. After an election, mountains of materials, including all the used ballots, are returned to Elections Canada in Ottawa to be stored. And the CEO must prepare a report for Parliament. Then it's time to get ready for another election!

He or She?

In 1993, Kim Campbell became the first woman prime minister of Canada. However, in this book the pronoun "he" has been used to refer to the position. In honour of Canada's first woman governor general, Jeanne Sauvé, appointed in 1984, the pronoun "she" is used to refer to the governor general.

Who Calls an Election?

Federal elections must be held at least once every five years. That is the law. But sometimes the prime minister doesn't wait that long. Instead, the prime minister calls an election when he thinks his party is most popular. (Popularity means votes.)

The prime minister must have the governor general's consent to call an election. He asks her to dissolve Parliament and to inform the chief electoral officer of the election day.

The prime minister can choose whatever date he wishes for election day. He will naturally choose a time when his party looks especially good to the public so his party candidates will have a good chance of being elected.

The prime minister will also likely wait until major bills he wants passed have been voted on. He can call the election for any time when he has a good chance of winning. The prime minister's choice of election day is passed on to the governor general who then informs the chief electoral officer.

A federal election may also be called if there is a "vote of non-confidence" in Parliament. This means that the government is defeated in the House of Commons because the members (representing their voters) no longer feel the government is working well. If the government loses the election, it is replaced; if it wins, it continues in office until the next federal election is held.

Get on the List!

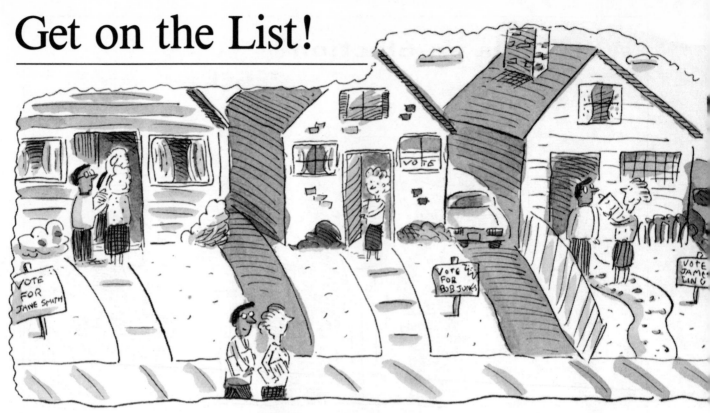

SUPPOSE YOU WANT TO TAKE SWIMMING LESSONS. Or maybe you enjoy music and you'd like to attend guitar classes. Chances are you'll have to register beforehand to make sure you can take part in the classes. The same thing happens when you are eligible to vote. Your name has to appear on the list of voters, called the register of electors.

Before the 1997 election, pairs of specially trained people called enumerators tried to visit every household in Canada during the electoral period to draw up a list of voters. They asked questions about citizenship and age. They wanted to make sure that people were eligible to vote.

The time and cost of sending thousands of enumerators across Canada was eliminated when a new system for collecting voter information was put in place in 1997. The register of electors is an automated data base of qualified voters. It contains each voter's name, mailing address, municipal address, electoral district, gender and date of birth.

The register can be updated using existing federal, territorial and provincial data, such as tax and driver's licence information. When you turn 18, you will be automatically included in the next register. No enumerator has to come to your home and put you on a list.

Government data also help Elections Canada find and include voters who are new citizens or who have moved from one electoral district to another. Voters' names are removed when they die. And the privacy of each voter is protected by law.

By the time election day arrives, there is one register of electors for each polling station. You can vote only at the polling station where your name appears on the register. If a voter's name is accidentally left off the register of electors, he or she can still register any time during the election period, including on election day.

An Unusual Map

A North Poll

The most northerly poll in Canada is in the new territory, Nunavut. The Nunavut riding covers more than three million square kilometres, but has a population of only 25,000. Voters receive their election materials by air — ballots and boxes are dropped by parachute! You could say it's the North Poll. Ho, ho, ho.

YOU'VE SEEN A MAP OF CANADA, RIGHT? BUT HAVE you ever seen an *electoral* map?

This kind of map divides Canada's 10 million square kilometres into 301 electoral districts, sometimes called ridings or constituencies.

If you look at an electoral map, you'll notice that all the electoral districts are not the same size. Why is this?

The country is divided according to the number and location of the people. Each province is allotted a certain number of seats. In 1997, Saskatchewan, for example, had 14 seats, while Ontario, because of its greater population, had 103. Less populated provinces, whether large or small, have fewer seats: Prince Edward Island elects four members and Nunavut, the Northwest Territories and Yukon send one each. As the population moves from one province to another or from one area in a province to another, the boundaries have to be changed. In 1996, the boundaries changed in 270 of the 301 electoral districts.

Sometimes an electoral district will grow larger; this means more travel for the candidates who will be campaigning there. The candidates in Nunavut (see page 18) will wear out more shoes covering the riding than the lucky candidates in Quebec's Laurier–Sainte-Marie riding, where 96,640 people live in only nine square kilometres.

Polling stations are located within each electoral district so that each poll takes care of about 350 voters. The voters in each electoral district vote for one of the candidates running for election in their area. In the next district, voters vote for different candidates, and so on across the country until all 301 electoral districts have new members to send to Parliament.

Have You Seen My Gerrymander?

In the past, there have been some famous scams concerning electoral district boundaries. One of the most famous happened around 1812 in the United States, when Elbridge Gerry was the governor of Massachusetts.

While Gerry was in office, the boundaries of some electoral districts were redrawn so that his party was sure to win. On the map, the new boundary lines formed the shape of a salamander's body. Someone said it should be called a "gerrymander." Since the boundary changes were illegal, the new word was not meant as a compliment for Governor Gerry.

Today, we use the word "gerrymandering" to mean the redrawing of riding boundaries to ensure votes for one party. This is a way of fixing the vote and is illegal. Thanks to the Electoral Boundaries Readjustment Act of 1964, gerrymandering is just about extinct in Canada.

You might be accused of gerrymandering on your next birthday if you're seen cutting around those icing roses to make sure your best friend gets plenty of them. Beware!

19

Let's Have a Party!

WHAT DO YOU THINK OF WHEN YOU HEAR THE word "party"? Balloons, plenty of fantastic food, music and friends? You can find all of these things during an election, but you'll also find other kinds of parties — *political* parties.

In the early days of Canadian history there were no political parties. Before 1810, each candidate asked the voters to support him alone, not a party. But gradually, during the 1800s, political parties were formed, with each party reflecting the shared beliefs of its members. Regional needs, religious beliefs and social class helped determine which party you belonged to. The reasons for creating new political parties change through history, but the goals remain the same. The joint efforts of party members help get their candidates elected. In Canada, the Conservative, Liberal and New Democratic parties, the Bloc Québécois and the Canadian Alliance have all played important parts in federal elections.

- We inherited the Conservative Party from England, where the party members were originally called Tories. The Tory Party was founded in 1689, and it supported the authority of government and opposed religious liberty. Times change and so do politics. In 1830, the name Tory was changed to Conservative. Canada's first prime minister, John A. Macdonald, was a member of the Conservative Party.

- The Liberal Party also began in England, where members were originally called Whigs. In Canada, party members were called Reformers, but after Confederation in 1867 they became known as the Liberals. The first Liberal prime minister was Alexander Mackenzie (1873). The Liberal Party has dominated federal politics during the last 100 years.

- The New Democratic Party (NDP) is a descendant of the Co-operative Commonwealth Federation (CCF), a party that was founded in Alberta in 1932. Early CCF members believed that government money should be more fairly distributed to poor Canadians. But some people were afraid of the CCF because they thought it was a Communist party. The party gained more support in 1961, when it renamed itself the New Democratic Party.
- The Bloc Québécois was born in 1990, when some members of Parliament resigned from the Conservative Party because they disagreed with that party's plans for Quebec. They organized themselves as the Bloc and ran candidates for the first time in the 1993 federal election.
- The Reform Party was born in Western Canada in 1987, when some voters became dissatisfied with the existing political parties and decided to take a new political path. The new party quickly gained strength. In the 1997 federal elections, the Reform Party became the official Opposition and, in 2000, was renamed the Canadian Reform Conservative Alliance (commonly known as the Canadian Alliance).

Most candidates support the beliefs and share the goals of a political party, but some candidates choose not to belong to a particular party and run as independents. MPs who are party members are usually expected to support their party's position when they vote in the House of Commons. But independent MPs may vote as they wish.

The Social Credit Party

The Great Depression also gave Canada the Social Credit Party, in 1932. Members of this party wanted to give away money (called social credit) so people could buy items and services. The buyers would be supporting businesses and keeping the economy going. The party is still active in British Columbia.

Watch Out! There's a Rhino at the Polls!

In many elections in Canada there have been other parties with candidates running for office. The Natural Law Party, Action Canada, the Communist Party of Canada and the Reconstruction Party have all fielded candidates. There have even been Rhinoceros Party candidates.

The Rhinoceros Party was started in Montreal in 1963 by people who wanted to poke fun at election campaigns. A rhino is thick-skinned, clumsy and stupid but can move fast when it senses danger. Rhino Party members thought this description fit a lot of politicians.

Rhino candidates sometimes dressed as clowns and the party's platforms were unusual. During some elections Rhinos promised the use of nuclear-powered toothbrushes, wanted to move the Rockies to Central Canada and asked for the repeal of the law of gravity. From 1963 to 1984, Rhino candidates participated in all of Canada's federal elections. In 1984, believe it or not, 99,207 Canadians voted for Rhino candidates.

The Rhinoceros Party is not an official party any more, but it still appears in the news at election time. In 1993, the joke-rich but cash-poor party urged voters to "Vote for Yourselves" – or write in their own names on the ballot.

The Parti Québécois

The Parti Québécois started in Quebec in 1968, mainly because many French Canadians wanted independence from the rest of Canada. The Parti Québécois pushed for sovereignty association for the province. This meant that Quebec would have a status equal to that of the Government of Canada. René Lévesque was the leader of the party. Although Parti Québécois candidates were elected to Quebec's parliament, the National Assembly, and had lots of support, the question of sovereignty association was rejected by the voters in 1980 in a referendum.

Don't Kick Sand!

Sometimes we say that somebody has "real grit." Grit (American slang) means determination, stamina. In Canadian politics, members of the Liberal Party were called Clear-Grits in the 1880s. Since grit is also a bit of dirt or sand, the name gave party members a nasty image. Like sand in your eyes, the Liberals were considered pure nuisances by the Conservatives.

Parliament

LET'S SAY YOU'VE ELECTED BOB BAYOBAB TO Parliament. What exactly is Parliament and what's Bob going to do there?

Parliament is something we've inherited from England. Long ago, English kings ruled with the help of a group of nobles called the Witan. These men made the laws and gave the king money and manpower. Later, kings found they needed more money than the Witan could provide and they called upon the rest of their subjects to help. Of course, *all* the people in England couldn't go to the king. Representatives were sent and they formed the parts of the

British Parliament: the House of Lords (the nobles) and the House of Commons (the "common" men).

Canada's Parliament is based on the English model. It consists of two parts, the House of Commons and the Senate. Members of the House of Commons are elected by voters. Senators are appointed by the prime minister. Some people argue that Senators should be *elected*, rather than *appointed*.

What's Bob Bayobab going to do in Parliament?

First he'll head for the House of Commons, the house he's been elected to serve in. Members of Parliament, called MPs for short, serve their riding constituents by attending daily sessions of Parliament. Bob will ask questions, debate issues such as acid rain and vote on laws. MPs also serve on committees that examine certain issues in detail. For example, Bob sits on the pollution committee. As well, MPs help their constituents needing assistance or advice. If he's doing his job well, Bob will be very busy looking after your interests while he's in Ottawa.

Who's on Left?

When you listen to people talking politics, you'll hear the directions "left" and "right" used. What on earth do these directions have to do with government?

During the French Revolution (1789–1799), King Louis XVI held meetings with the citizens. The nobles sat on the king's right at the table, while the priests and middle classes sat on his left. (You'll notice the lower classes were not represented at all, hence the Revolution!)

After the overthrow of King Louis, the government followed the same general pattern. Members who supported tradition sat on the right, and those who supported equality sat on the left. Today, some people say that the Canadian Alliance is on the right, the New Democratic Party is on the left, and the other parties are in between.

Majority/Minority

After an election you will hear the words "majority" and "minority" a lot. The party that elects the most candidates is asked by the governor general to form a government. If the government party wins more than half the seats, it is called a *majority government*.

In a majority government it is a lot easier for the government to get what it wants. Think about it. You and nine of your pizza-loving friends have enough money to buy one large pizza. If the *majority* of your friends love anchovies but you don't, you can be sure you'll be picking anchovies off your slice! You're outnumbered.

Some people say a majority government can get spoiled and lazy because it doesn't need to win support from other parties; it automatically gets what it wants. Constant examination and questioning by the other parties help keep the government attentive to the needs of the voters.

A *minority government* is formed when the government has fewer than half the seats but more seats than any

other single party. Minority governments often have a difficult time. The other parties can join forces and vote against everything the government wants. To keep this from happening, the government has to work harder to convince the other parties.

Bob may take on more responsibilities, too. If his party forms the government, he may be asked by the prime minister to take a position in the *Cabinet*. This special group of ministers looks after the various government departments. The prime minister decides who gets which department, and the ministers act as advisors to him. (Bob is being considered for Minister of the Environment because he's had so much to say about pollution.)

Talk, Talk, Talk

The word "parliament" comes from the Latin word "parliamentum," which means "to talk." When you watch the parliamentary debates on television, you'll notice that members *do* talk a lot! They present ideas, argue back and forth and sometimes even swear. Their words, even the naughty ones, are taken down for history — and for you. This record of what has been said is called *Hansard* after T. C. Hansard, the printer of the British parliamentary debates from 1812 until 1892.

Parliamentarians are talkative! A year's worth of talk in the Ontario legislature takes up an average of 8,000 pages in *Hansard*. One year, Ontario MPPs filled 20,000 pages.

Who keeps track of all those words?

In the House of Commons, the debates are digitally recorded. Transeditors then listen to the debates through their computer terminals. The material is edited and prepared for printing. By the next morning, a completed copy of everything said is printed in both official languages and ready to be read. *Hansard* is also available on the Parliamentary Internet site (http://www.parl.gc.ca).

You can read through *Hansard* and find out what Bob Bayobab has said about certain issues. Then you can decide whether or not to support his re-election.

If Bob's party comes second in the election, he'll be in the Opposition. His party leader may ask Bob to be in the *Shadow Cabinet*. For example, Bob may be selected to "shadow" the Minister of the Environment. He'll be expected to keep up to date on environmental issues and aim questions at the minister while Parliament is in session.

Watch Out for Mrs. Smith!

IN MOST GROUPS THERE'S SOMEONE WHO DECIDES to disregard the rules and do his or her own thing. Maybe Jonas takes two Cokes when he's been asked to keep it to one. Maybe Kate takes a look at your paper during the exam. They don't think they're hurting anyone — maybe they're just not thinking at all. But the rules are there for a reason. If people take two Cokes, there won't be enough for everyone; if Kate gets an unusually high test score and the marks are done on a curve, your grade may be lower than it would have been. You've been cheated!

Cheating (fraud) can take place during an election, too. No one likes to admit it does, but it does. Close monitoring by electoral officials keeps the cheating in check. But some people, like Mrs. Smith, are very determined to do whatever it takes to get their candidate elected.

Ballot stuffing — Mrs. Smith steals ballots and votes more than once in the election.

Telegraphing — Heavily disguised (she thinks she's an actress!), Mrs. Smith goes to the polling station and pretends to be Mrs. Jones, who is a registered voter.

Treating — Mrs. Smith, with more money than brains, offers a few dollars to John Doe. But there's a hitch. John Doe has to vote for Mrs. Smith's candidate. Today such bribery is not found too often simply because it is very expensive. And with a secret ballot, how will Mrs. Smith know if John voted for her choice?

False enumeration — Mrs. Smith tampers with the voters' list. She decides to take off the name of any voter she knows will vote against her candidate. She also adds

During elections in the 1940s, women were bribed with stockings because hosiery was so scarce during World War II.

the names of under-age voters, including a few babies. She'll vote in their place. (Remember the Toronto dog who almost voted?)

Brute force — Mrs. Smith has been known to batter a voter with her umbrella in order to "convince" him to change his vote.

It goes without saying — anyone who participates in these types of fraud will be prosecuted. Watch out, Mrs. Smith!

Denied the Right to Vote!

Imagine you've just turned 18 and you're excited about voting. The election has been called and you know your name is on the register of electors. This is it! It's election day! You're at the polling station, ready to make your mark.

"Oh, I'm sorry," the clerk says. "You said your name is Sylvia Chang?"

"Yes," you answer proudly, waiting for any other questions.

"Yes, dear? Well, I *am* sorry," says a nearby officer. "You're of Chinese ancestry, so you can't vote. Maybe the laws will change before the next election."

Today the idea of being discriminated against just because of your ancestry seems crazy. There are laws to make sure it can't happen. But not too long ago, voter discrimination was a fact in Canada.

The Chinese

During the 1800s, many Chinese labourers were brought to Canada to lay the tracks for Canada's transcontinental railroad. They worked long hours in dangerous conditions. Prime Minister John A. Macdonald, a chief promoter of the railroad, said the Chinese were fine in Canada as labourers, but it would be unfortunate if they became permanent residents and had the right to vote.

Imagine if all blond Canadians more than six feet tall were denied the right to vote! The government would be pressured by citizens to change its stand right away. But many Canadians shared Macdonald's beliefs, and Asians were not allowed to vote for many years. Chinese Canadians and East Indian Canadians gained the vote in federal and provincial elections in 1947. The first Chinese-Canadian MP was elected in 1957.

Native Peoples

Native peoples living on Canadian reserves were not allowed to vote in a federal election until 1960, about the time your parents were children. The right to vote in *provincial* elections came even later for some Native peoples. Those on reserves in Alberta got the provincial vote in 1965; in Quebec, the Native peoples have voted in provincial elections for only the last 20 years. That's about 200 years after the first votes were cast in Canada!

The Inuit were ignored by the government until 1939 — and they still did not get the vote until 1950. Now Inuit are active in local, territorial and federal politics.

The Japanese

The Japanese came to Canada in the late 1800s and settled mainly on the west coast. They were denied the right to vote even though they were very active members of Canadian society.

The sons and daughters of these immigrants were born in Canada but they were still denied the vote simply because of their culture. During World War II, when Canada joined the war against Germany and Japan, the Japanese Canadians were placed in internment camps. Their property was taken by the Canadian government and was not returned, even after the war was over. (A good story about a family in the camps is *Naomi's Road* by Joy Kogawa.)

These people were punished only because they shared a heritage with the enemy. It wasn't until 1949, after the war, that Japanese Canadians were granted the right to vote.

The Mennonites

A similar kind of discrimination happened to the Mennonites during World War I. The Mennonites were members of a religious sect, centred in Germany, who came to America in the 1700s. Many settled in Manitoba and Southern Ontario.

After Britain declared war on Germany in 1914, the Mennonites were accused of being spies for Germany, just because they spoke German. The government took away their right to vote in the 1917 election and didn't restore it until the 1920s. Imagine having the vote for one election and then having it taken away in the next!

Today, some Old Order Mennonites are opposed to holding public office, but others, like the Conference Mennonites, run for and win public offices.

Thank You, Nurses!

IF IT WEREN'T FOR THE NURSES WHO RISKED THEIR lives in World War I, Canadian women might still be waiting for the right to vote. Before the war the saying, "No woman, idiot, lunatic or criminal shall vote" outraged women. One politician asked, "What in the world do women want to vote for?... My mother was the best woman in the world and she certainly never wanted to vote!"

Around 1910, Canadian women started to demand the vote. Women who spoke out and battled for the right to vote were called *suffragettes*. (Suffrage, like *franchise*, is the right or privilege of voting.) Meetings of suffragettes and their supporters were held all over the world. The result? Riots, arrests, prison and for some, death.

Then came the war. Conscription, or the compulsory drafting of men into the armed forces, was the major issue in the 1917 election. Prime Minister Robert Borden wanted to make sure that his government and its conscription plans got the voters' support. He thought the patriotic women nurses overseas would back him, so he gave them the vote. To be safe, Borden took the vote away from foreign-born Canadians, unless they had a son, grandson, or brother serving in battle and instead gave the vote to the wives, mothers and sisters of servicemen. Women were allowed to vote in a federal election for the first time. You can guess what happened. Borden and his government won the election.

During the war, people who were against the idea of women voting began to change their minds. Thousands of men left their jobs and went to Europe to fight. That left women with extra responsibilities. They had to keep their homes and families going *and* they had to work outside the home to help the war effort and keep Canada going. People began to feel that women deserved a say in how the government worked.

Now You Have It, Now You Don't

X SOME WOMEN IN THE MARITIMES AND QUEBEC HAD the vote in the late 1700s and early 1800s, but lost the vote later: after Confederation in 1867 men could vote and women no longer could. (When the right to vote is taken away it is called *disenfranchisement*.) The same Sir John A. Macdonald who denied the Chinese citizenship tried to get the vote for women in the 1880s. But he failed. By 1900, Canadian women could vote in municipal elections and become school trustees in some cities. But they were still denied a vote for the government of Canada.

Three strong women battled over the years for the Canadian woman's right to vote in every election and to hold office. Of course, they weren't the only supporters of women's rights, but they were among the most outspoken. They appeared at government meetings, wrote for newspapers and made public appearances. Radio and, later, television gave McClung, Macphail and Casgrain maximum exposure to the people, and helped these women bring about something quite extraordinary — the chance for every woman to help shape Canada's government.

Nellie McClung (1873 - 1951)

Nellie Mooney McClung was born in Ontario but grew up in Manitoba. She began to teach school when she was 16 and later wrote books. McClung married a druggist and together they raised five children. Still she had time to work in a temperance society (a group that tried to stop the sale of alcoholic beverages). After her family moved to Winnipeg in 1911, McClung found she was invited to speak more often about women's suffrage, and after yet another family move, to Edmonton, she continued her

NELLIE McCLUNG

fight for women's rights.

McClung served as a member of the legislative assembly for five years before moving to Vancouver and continuing her suffrage efforts. She was a humorous, convincing public speaker who was never afraid to challenge politicians.

Agnes Macphail (1890 - 1954)

Agnes Campbell Macphail was the first woman elected to the federal House of Commons after Canadian women gained the right to vote. She served in the House from 1921 until 1940 and in 1943 became one of the first women elected to the Ontario legislature.

Like McClung, Macphail was born in Ontario and taught school when she was very young. Her political career included being a founder of the CCF Party in 1932. Agnes Macphail worked hard for prison reform, farm issues and equal pay legislation. She died just before her appointment to the Senate was announced.

AGNES MACPHAIL   THÉRÈSE CASGRAIN

Thérèse Casgrain (1896 - 1981)

Women voters in Quebec owe a great deal of thanks to Thérèse Forget Casgrain. She was born to a wealthy family in Montreal, married a lawyer and raised four children. She was a founding member of the Provincial Franchise Committee in 1921 and helped Québécois women get the right to vote provincially in 1940. Thérèse Casgrain was provincial leader of the CCF Party in the 1950s and was appointed to the Senate in 1970.

Steps in the Right Direction

1916 Manitoba becomes the first province to allow women to vote in provincial elections. Saskatchewan and Alberta follow.

1917 The Military Voters Act gives war nurses the federal vote. The Wartime Elections Act grants the vote to wives, mothers and sisters of servicemen. Ontario and British Columbia grant women provincial voting rights.

1918 Women aged 21 and older are granted the right to vote in federal elections.

1919 Women can stand for seats in the House of Commons.

1940 Quebec becomes the last province to give women the vote.

Lessons from History

FASCINATING PICTURES OF LIFE LONG AGO CAN BE found in old newspapers, poll books and political pamphlets from past elections. Old poll books, usually kept in a town or city hall, are lists of voters and their addresses and occupations. Take the City of Toronto Poll Book for 1841, for example.

Each voter is identified by his occupation. (You'll only see the names of the men; women weren't allowed to vote yet.) There were blacksmiths and whitesmiths. (A whitesmith is a worker in "white iron," or tin.) Toronto in 1841 had 90 builders and carpenters, one undertaker (listed under carpenters) and eight ministers. Three people made soap and candles for the city and kept light in the taverns run by 67 tavern keepers. Only seven male teachers served all the children who were allowed to go to school and nine coach-makers, wagon-makers and wheel-wrights kept Toronto moving. If you were wealthy enough to buy a piano there was only one man who could build it. Some of the voters' names will bring a smile to your face. Charles Clinkinbroomer was a watch-maker with a great name!

After each name there are the initials of the candidates for whom the man voted. You could look at the poll book and see who your neighbourhood butcher voted for. If it wasn't *your* candidate, you might take your business to another butcher.

According to the poll book, voting lasted for seven days, instead of one day as it does today, and the tally for each day's vote was recorded. If your candidate was losing on Tuesday, you could try to drum up support for the other voting days.

A Ballot with a Beer Chaser

Long ago, the local tavern was a general meeting place for the neighbourhood, so it was only natural that voting should take place there. Tables were set up outside the tavern for the election.

Finding supporters could be an expensive, sometimes nasty business. Servants were sometimes forced by their employers to vote for certain candidates. Bribery of tavern keepers was common and there was always lots of whiskey around to keep voters happy. A vote could be bought for the price of a whiskey punch. When the final votes were tallied, the victorious candidate was sometimes hoisted on a tavern chair above the heads of his supporters and carried around the town. Imagine the noise of the celebrating winners and the drinking done by the losers who wanted to forget the election. Often, there were riots between the two groups and sometimes innocent bystanders were killed during the scuffles.

An election in Montreal in 1832 left a man named François Languedoc dead on the street. Newspapermen saw Languedoc's death as a reason to stay home during an election. They reported:

"Languedoc yielded to the repeated importunities of his friends and went to the poll. He had never made a practice of attending elections and was a

remarkably peaceful man; but in an unfortunate moment went to the poll on Monday, arrived at the time of the riot and in a few minutes he was numbered with the dead."

Laws that curbed the riots were eventually passed. During the hours a polling station was open for a provincial election, no one could buy liquor. This law was abolished in 1975 because it was outdated — politicians were not buying votes with liquor any more.

See How They Run

Come to the Toga Party!

The word *candidate* comes from the Latin word meaning "clothed in white." Why? Long ago in ancient Rome, men who wished to be elected or appointed to office wore white togas. Imagine if modern-day candidates dressed in white togas on election day!

ONCE A FEDERAL ELECTION HAS BEEN CALLED AND an election day is set, the countdown begins. There is a minimum of 36 days before people vote and there's plenty to be done. Election day is called "Day 0" and "Day 21" is Nomination Day. On that day, a list with the names of every candidate in Canada is drawn up.

How do candidates get nominated?

Any person who is a qualified voter can run for office. The candidate may seek election in only one electoral district at a time.

A candidate who wants to represent a political party must win the support of that party: this is usually done at a nomination meeting held by party members in the electoral district. A candidate who is not endorsed by a party can run as an independent candidate. But that's only the beginning.

Let's say Tiffany Lampe wants to be an MP for the Edisonville district. She must have an official agent (who handles all the financial transactions of the campaign) and an auditor (someone who will check financial reports). The returning officer in the district will give Tiffany official nomination papers. To be nominated officially in most ridings, she needs at least 100 signatures of voters who live in the Edisonville district. All Tiffany's nomination papers must be completed and turned in by 2 P.M. on Day 21. She also needs to make a money deposit to show she's serious about running for office.

At the end of Day 21, if Tiffany is the only candidate, the returning officer will close the election and declare her the winner by *acclamation*.

It was easy for Tiffany, wasn't it? For most candidates there's a great deal more work.

Let's say two other people decide to run against Tiffany Lampe. She'll have to campaign to win voters' support. She'll choose a *campaign manager* to oversee every detail of her campaign. Tiffany will need someone who has a lot of campaign experience. The manager will see that a headquarters is set up, maybe in a vacant store. He or she will make sure Tiff gets to the opening of that new seniors' centre and that she has her picture taken kissing a cute baby. It's important for Tiffany to be known by voters. The manager will also arrange fund-raising dinners so the money will keep coming in and will hire speech-writers to help Tiffany present her ideas well to the voters.

Campaigning is hard work. Tiffany will have to go

Wanderlust

Prime Minister Sir Wilfrid Laurier was the first party leader ever to visit the western provinces during a federal campaign. That was in 1917, and he travelled by train. Candidates now need a faster way of getting around so they fly thousands of kilometres to see voters in hard-to-reach parts of Canada. Sir John A. Macdonald might have seen a thousand voters during a campaign; today's politicians see hundreds of thousands in just a few weeks.

TIFFANY LAMPE

ELECTION HEADQUARTERS

mainstreeting: she'll stroll through shopping malls or down busy streets in her area, shaking hands and chatting with voters. She wants to get to know the voters and let them get to know her. What are their concerns? How can she help them?

By the time Tiffany Lampe is elected, she may have gained 5 kilograms (11 pounds) from too much fast food and too many benefit dinner banquets. She may have dark circles under her eyes from lack of sleep after late-night speeches. And her family may hardly recognize her because she's hardly been home. But it's all part of a candidate's life and Tiffany Lampe hopes that on election day her efforts will result in victory.

Slogans

When you urge your school team on to victory at the hockey play-offs, you cheer, "Go get 'em, Rivercrest!" or whatever your school is called. This slogan whips up team spirit. Election slogans work the same way. Long ago slogans were the battle cries of warriors; now slogans appear on election posters, television commercials and buttons.

Here are some slogans from past elections:

"By a Party, with a Party, but for a Country" (Sir John A. Macdonald, 1875)

"Let Laurier Finish His Work" (Sir Wilfrid Laurier, 1908)
"King or Chaos" (William Lyon Mackenzie King, 1935)
"Peace, Progress and Pearson" (Lester Pearson, 1957)
"Trudeau and One Canada" (Pierre Elliot Trudeau, 1968)

Notice that the name of the candidate is usually part of the slogan. Some candidates today hire advertising agencies to create election slogans that will keep their names in the voters' minds right until election day.

"Getting to Know You..."

WHEN TIFFANY LAMPE ANNOUNCED HER CANDIDACY in your riding, maybe you'd never heard of her before. Why should you give her your vote? She's just a name to you. How can you get more information about her?

Choosing a candidate can be difficult. Candidates from different political parties often say basically the same thing. After all, no candidate is going to say he or she doesn't care about acid rain. Listen carefully. Tiffany may propose a quick solution. Mr. C. may say acid rain is not a top priority issue; the budget is his concern.

How do you find out what candidates stand for? Political parties and candidates print pamphlets that outline key election topics. They maintain sites on the Internet and distribute "video brochures" that introduce the candidate and the party's platform.

Local and national newspapers are filled with articles and editorials about candidates and what they think. And television can let you see some parliamentarians in action. If Mr. C. is running for re-election, you may want to see how he performs daily in Ottawa, on television. You might also read what he's said in *Hansard* (see page 27).

You can also talk to Tiffany face to face. Candidates visit neighbourhoods to talk to the voters. Tiffany may knock on your door or attend a community picnic. That's your chance to ask her what she really feels about issues of concern to you.

Building a New Government

A *plank* of the candidate's platform is a single item of the party's plan of action. Solutions for the homeless, for example, might be one major plank of a candidate's platform.

These building words remind us of the early days of campaigning when politicians stood on wooden platforms high above the crowds and delivered fiery speeches.

If you want to see how Tiffany's ideas compare to those of other candidates, go to an all-candidates meeting. Voters can listen to speeches by all of the candidates in the area and ask questions. Ready to decide? Which candidate will receive your vote on Day 0?

Run for the Money

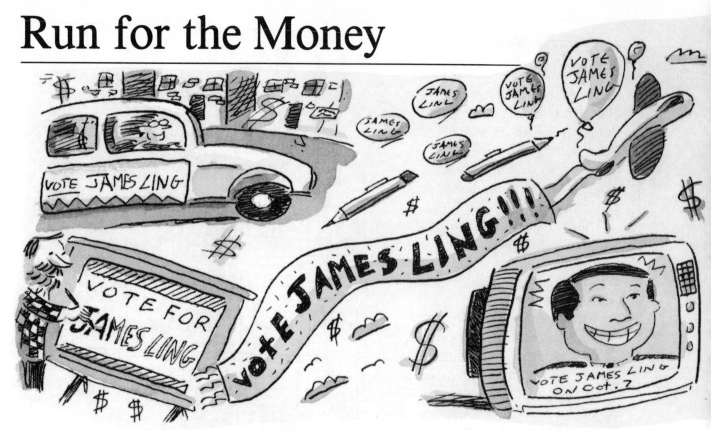

IT TAKES A LOT OF MONEY TO RUN A CAMPAIGN.
There are offices to maintain, cars and chairs to
rent, paper-clips, pens, stickers to buy, signs and
brochures to print and people to hire. Even grocery items
like coffee and sugar have to be figured into the cost of a
campaign. Volunteer supporters do much of the work but
still there are bills, bills, bills.

What would happen if a very wealthy candidate ran
against a poor one? Wouldn't the wealthy one have a
better chance of winning because he or she could buy
more television ads or larger signs?

Not necessarily.

By law, candidates and their parties can spend only a
certain amount on an election campaign. These spending
limits are determined by the number of voters in each
candidate's riding. In large ridings, candidates are granted
extra funds because of the high cost of travel.

The political parties also have limits to what they can
spend. These limits are based on the number of voters in

the ridings in which they are running candidates. The largest
parties can spend over $10 million each.

After the election, parties and candidates must reveal
the source of campaign contributions. They must identify
any person or group who gives more than $100 to a party
in any given year or to a candidate in an election.
Otherwise, someone might try to slip a few extra million
dollars to a candidate in return for future favours.

Perhaps your family wants to contribute big bucks to a
particular party or candidate. If you want to fill a suitcase
with shiny loonies and lug it down to your candidate's office,
you can. But you'll have to get an official receipt for all that
cash. What will you get in return for your money? Forget
about special favours. Instead, you'll get a tax credit from
the government. This "reward" encourages voters to give
more than votes to the candidates they admire.

Animal Farm

Listen to the radio during an election and you might think you've stumbled into a barnyard. You'll hear about ducks, dogs, lambs and horses. Here's a guide to who's who.

Dark Horse
Sometimes people believe a candidate has no chance at all of winning. Then on election day, surprise! In horse racing, the same thing happens. Most of the bets have been placed on, say, Greased Lightning, but Old Fred wins the race. The candidate who comes "from nowhere" and wins the election is the dark horse.

The horse-racing expression "running neck-and-neck" is also used during a campaign or on election day. It means the candidates are within a few votes of each other.

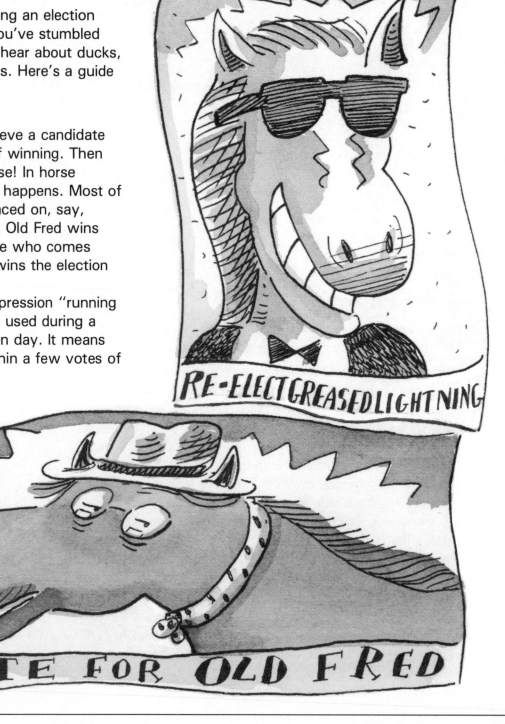

Sacrificial Lamb

If a very popular candidate is running for re-election, the chances of beating her may be slim. A candidate who runs against her is almost sure to lose. He or she is a "sacrificial lamb."

Why be a sacrificial lamb? To gain experience and perhaps be rewarded by the party with an appointment or support in another election.

Underdog

During a campaign, voters are sometimes asked their opinion about who will win. The results of these *public opinion polls* let people know who is in the lead before election day. The "underdog" is the losing party or candidate. Just because a candidate is called the underdog a few weeks before election day doesn't mean he or she will lose the election. Voters can change their minds right up until they mark their ballots!

Lame Duck

A prime minister who announces he's retiring can expect to be called a lame duck. He is still in power, but everyone knows he's on the way out. Voters don't pay as much attention to a politician in this position, so it's more difficult for him to get things done. Like a duck who can't fly, he is unable to make any progress. Voters are looking ahead to the next prime minister, who they hope will give them what they want and need.

Pork-barrelling

This is when members of government give out jobs or contracts to supporters rather than to others who might be better qualified or more deserving. Sometimes, this is how sacrificial lambs are rewarded. Pork-barrelling is also called political patronage.

"How Do I Look?"

X WHEN YOU GO TO APPLY FOR A JOB AT THE hardware store, you don't spray your hair green, and wear a ripped T-shirt — and expect to get the job. You dress for success. First impressions are important in elections too, and candidates spend lots of time and money "improving their images" before meeting voters.

Television brings candidates into voters' living rooms. Candidates who "look bad" on TV hire media experts to groom them for appearances. Some candidates get complete make-overs, everything from a new hairdo and contact lenses to a snappier wardrobe.

Political parties produce television commercials that are broadcast during the final weeks before election day. But such advertising is banned the day before election day — and on the day itself.

Some candidates have trademarks — certain items that become identified with them. Prime Minister Lester Pearson wore bow-ties, Prime Minister Pierre Trudeau often sported a rose in his lapel and Ontario Premier David Peterson wore red neckties. These trademarks help politicians set themselves apart from the rest of the pack and give you something to remember.

JOHN A. MACDONALD

WILFRID LAURIER

BRIAN MULRONEY

Funny Faces

Sometimes it's part of a candidate's face that becomes his or her trademark. For example, Prime Minister Brian Mulroney was known for his chin. During elections, political cartoonists fill editorial pages with their funny, but meaningful, comments on the candidates and events. These caricatures exaggerate a candidate's facial features and can replace the real image of the person in people's minds.

Political cartooning has been going on for hundreds, maybe even thousands, of years. Canada's first prime minister, Sir John A. Macdonald, was caricatured weekly by cartoonist J.W. Bengough. For many people today, Bengough's cartoon is still their picture of Macdonald. Bengough started his own magazine, filled with this kind of cartoon, and kept his readers laughing *and* informed about every bit of the prime minister's career. Check out the editorial page of your local paper — and be prepared to chuckle!

Say It Louder, Please!

The secret ballot is also called an Australian Ballot because the Australians pioneered its use in 1858.

A HUNDRED AND FIFTY YEARS AGO WHEN YOU voted (remember, only men could vote) you called the name of your choice *out loud* in front of the candidates and all of their supporters. An election clerk wrote down your choice. This method was called *viva voce*, Latin for "voting out loud." Because all voting was public, there were many opportunities for bullying and vote buying.

Merchants might say to customers who owed them money, "Vote for my man and we'll forget this debt." Or a candidate's supporters might try to buy voters by buying them drinks. In 1831, a man could buy a gallon of whiskey for only 20 cents and that could buy quite a few votes.

Back in 1831 a group of reformers wanted laws passed to clean up elections. They pushed for secret ballots — paper ballots on which the voter could write the name of his choice. (These reformers also wanted the poll locations to be closer to the people. In early days, voters had to travel for miles in poor weather on rough roads and at great expense. Because of this, many people never voted.)

Not everyone agreed with voting in secret. Some people believed it was sneaky. If you were committed to a candidate, they argued, why not proudly call out his name? Open voting was called "the manly British practice." But the reformers won. The secret ballot became law in 1874. The first secret ballot slid into a ballot box in the federal election of 1878.

Paper Power

Ballot is from an Italian word "ballotta," meaning a round bullet. In the 1500s in Venice, Italy, voters dropped a bullet-like ball into a box or urn marked with their candidate's name.

Today, millions of ballots are printed on official ballot paper. The paper contains a barely visible design called a watermark. This mark can be seen only when the paper is held to the light. It cannot be copied. If someone prints ballots on a paper without this watermark, election officials suspect tampering and destroy all the ballots. All ballots are numbered so that they can be identified and are kept under tight security before and after election day.

Voting Underwater and Under the Weather

VOTERS CAN FIND THEMSELVES IN SOME STRANGE situations on election day. What if you're in the hospital? Or in a submarine? Or out of the country? Can you still vote? Read on and find out.

You've had a sore throat for a few days and the doctor says your tonsils have to come out. The operation is scheduled for, you guessed it, election day! Don't worry — you can still vote. Advance polls are open several days before election day for those who are going to be away. And mobile polling stations travel to hospitals and nursing homes, enabling people who can't get to a regular polling station to vote with other Canadians on election day.

If you're living outside Canada or just across the country, away from your regular polling station, you can vote with a Special Ballot that you mail in. The ballot has a bar code to keep your vote secret — and to make sure that you vote only once. It comes with some simple, easy-to-follow instructions.

So don't worry if your tonsils act up or if your family has taken the year off to travel around Europe. Advance voting, a mobile polling station or a special ballot will enable you to vote. Even submarine crews and astronauts can cast their ballots. Hmmmm... a Special Ballot from Mars.

Other Special Cases

- Blind and visually impaired people can vote, even though they can't see the ballot. A piece of stiff paper (a template) is slipped over a ballot. The circles on the ballot match up with circles cut into the template. The voter feels these circles to find out where to make his or her mark. The poll official may be asked to tell the voter the order of the names on the ballot.
- Illiterate voters (those who can't read) or voters who are disabled (perhaps they cannot use their hands) can bring a friend to help them vote. Special oaths are taken and the voter and friend can then go to the booth together to mark the ballot or the deputy returning officer can help the voter.
- Elections Canada prints materials in more than 30 languages — including several aboriginal languages — so that Canadians of all ancestries can find out how to vote. A voter may ask for help from an interpreter at the polling station, but the interpreter cannot go behind the screen where the ballot is marked.

Election Day at Last!

Whoops!

If you accidentally rip your ballot or mark it incorrectly, you'll be given a new one. The officer will write "spoiled" on the ripped ballot and will keep it apart from the other ballots in the ballot box. Ballots are rejected if there are two marks on them instead of one, or if there is writing over the candidate's name, instead of in the circle. As long as there is a single mark in one circle only, the ballot is acceptable.

WEEKS OF WORK HAVE GONE INTO THE ELECTION and the polling stations are ready to open. Voters will be able to mark their ballots during specified local voting hours. No campaign literature or party supporters are allowed near or in the station; no one can put pressure on a voter as he or she enters to vote.

Let's imagine you're a first-time voter and walk through the voting procedure. You may be surprised at how simple it is!

As you enter the polling station, the first thing you'll see are two people sitting behind a table — the *deputy returning officer* (DRO) and a *poll clerk*. The poll clerk finds your name on the register of electors, marks it off and enters your name in the poll book record. The DRO is in charge at the polling station and gives you a folded ballot, which he or she has already initialled on the back. You'll then go behind a cardboard voting screen placed on a table.

Now what?

Listed on the ballot are the candidates' names and parties. The names are listed alphabetically. Beside each name is a blank circle. You will mark with an X one circle of the ballot and return it, folded, to the officer.

Forgot your pen? Don't worry. Pencils are provided at each voting screen.

When you hand your marked ballot back to the DRO, she checks to make sure it is the same ballot she gave you. She does this by looking at the initials she put on the ballot earlier. (Because of the way the ballot is folded, she does not see which candidate you marked.) Then she puts your ballot in the ballot box. Or you can do it yourself.

The poll clerk writes "voted" next to your name in the poll book. Congratulations! You have just finished voting for the first time!

Aaron Aardvark

Some people say that there is an advantage to being named Aaron Aardvark if you are running for office. Your name will be the first on the ballot. When there isn't a favourite candidate in an election, the first name on the ballot tends to get more votes!

Who Can Work at the Polls?

You may be interested in politics. Perhaps you're thinking about a career as a politician. You're 16 and you already have a job at Bobo's Burgers so you're certainly old enough to work at a polling station and learn how it all works.

Not so.

The people who are hired to work at polling stations have to be eligible voters, so they all have to be at least 18. Many people think this is unfair. They argue that if young people become more involved in government *before* they turn 18, they might be more interested in what is going on when they *can* vote.

There's hope that the age rules for polling-station workers will change and that young people will have more opportunities to get involved.

What? No Time to Vote?

Every voter in Canada is entitled to have three consecutive hours to vote on election day. This may involve taking some time off work. A boss cannot punish any worker who leaves to vote. But he may decide which three hours employees can be gone. All the nurses at a hospital can't leave at the same time to vote!

Scrutinizing the Situation

When you enter the polling station, you may see some people sitting near the DRO and the poll clerk. These are the *scrutineers*. They observe carefully, or "scrutinize," the voting proceedings to make sure everything is following the law.

Scrutineers are appointed by the candidates to work at the station on their behalf. They may examine the poll book as election day progresses to see who has voted. If John Green, one of the candidate's strongest supporters, hasn't voted yet, the scrutineer may relay information to the campaign office. People there can call Mr. Green and see if he needs a ride to the polls, a babysitter, whatever. They need his vote. A scrutineer can leave and re-enter the station as he pleases and can challenge a voter's right to vote. But he cannot question any voter or influence a voter's decision.

After the Doors Close

YOU'VE VOTED, SO YOUR WORK ON ELECTION DAY IS done. But there are others who keep working after the polling station doors are locked. That's when the vote counting starts.

The ballot box, which has been sealed shut during the day, is opened and all the ballots are emptied onto a table. Only the deputy returning officer (DRO) can handle the ballots and he or she is closely watched by the

DRO   SCRUTINEERS   POLL CLERK

LING   SMITH   LAMPE   KLEIN

scrutineers. The DRO picks up each ballot, checks the initials on the back and calls out the name of the candidate marked on it. The ballot is shown to the scrutineers and the poll clerk. A separate pile is kept for each candidate. Unmarked, rejected and spoiled ballots are also put into separate piles and counted.

The poll clerk and scrutineers keep score on the official tally sheets provided by Elections Canada. Ballots are rejected if a voter put two marks instead of one, or wrote over the candidate's name, not in the circles. The total number of ballots counted must equal the number of names registered by the clerk in the poll book.

To prevent voters from being influenced by early votes, the ballots from the advance polling days are not counted until the polls close on election day. The DRO counts these votes, too. In some municipal elections, computers tally the votes, but officials are finding problems with this method. Costly and frustrating recounts become necessary when the machines malfunction.

When the ballot count and the poll book count match, the DRO completes and certifies an official statement of the votes. The ballots are never counted again unless a recount is granted later. Each scrutineer is given a certificate of the count. A closing oath is taken by the poll officials and the documents are placed in the ballot box with all the ballots. The box is sealed with a new set of seals and taken or sent back to the returning officer. Meanwhile, the DROs at various polls phone in their results to the returning officer. The media and the people

Oh No! Not Again!

A recount may be held if the results are very close. In the case of a tie, the returning officer can vote and break the tie. (He may flip a coin to do this.) Otherwise the returning officer cannot vote.

It's Official!

After all the ballot boxes have been returned, the returning officer double checks the count on the official statements in each box. If there isn't a request for recount within seven days, the returning officer completes the election writ and notifies the chief electoral officer of the name of the winning candidate. A copy of the notice is given to each candidate. Candidates cannot be sworn in until the returning officer has sent the writ of election back to the chief electoral officer.

at party headquarters will soon know the final tabulations, but these will only be *unofficial* results.

After the winners are declared, reports have to be filed with Elections Canada. All the ballots, used and unused, are sent to Ottawa, where Elections Canada keeps them for one year. Then, old election materials are sent for recycling. Candidates, winners and losers, have to submit to the returning officer an account of all the money they spent and received for the transmission to Elections Canada. Constituency offices for the newly elected members of Parliament have to be staffed on a permanent basis. Newsletters and reports have to be printed and sent to voters.

And *your* job as a voter is not done yet either. Voters should listen to and watch the people they elected. After all, the winning candidates may decide to run for re-election in future. You'll need to know if they've done well. Being a watchdog is a full-time job.

Did you ever think you could do so much just by marking an X in a circle?

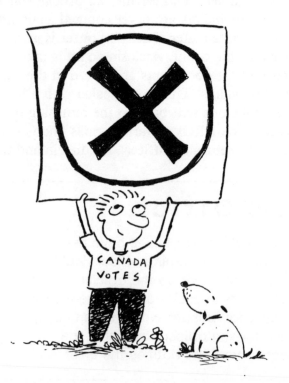

Glossary

acclamation This occurs when only one candidate files a nomination paper and is therefore declared the winner.

advance polls These polling stations open before election day so that voters in special circumstances can vote.

Australian ballot A secret ballot.

ballot The special piece of paper marked by a voter.

ballot stuffing Voting more than once in an election.

by-election A special election held between elections in order to fill vacant provincial or federal seats.

Cabinet A group of ministers who look after various government departments.

campaign manager The person who oversees a candidate's election plan and manages the details.

caricature A portrait in which the subject's features are deliberately exaggerated or distorted.

chief electoral officer (CEO) The government official who is in charge of co-ordinating all aspects of an election.

conscription The compulsory drafting of men into the armed forces.

constituents Voters in a riding who are represented by an elected official.

democracy Government by the people, either directly or through elected representatives.

deputy returning officer (DRO) An official at the polling station on election day.

disenfranchisement This occurs when the right to vote is taken away.

Elections Canada An agency of Parliament responsible for the organization of all federal elections.

electoral map A special map showing the electoral districts in a province or territory or across the country.

enumerators Representatives of political parties who went door to door and compiled the list of voters.

false enumeration Tampering with the voters' lists to "fix" the election outcome.

franchise The right or privilege to vote; also called suffrage.

Hansard The official printed record of all that is said during parliamentary debates.

House Assembly The provincial parliament of Newfoundland.

House of Commons One of the sections of Parliament. The members are elected by eligible voters; also called the Lower House.

Legislative Assembly The provincial parliament in some provinces.

majority government A majority government occurs when the winning party has more than half the seats in Parliament.

minority government A minority government is formed when the winning party has fewer than half the seats in Parliament but more seats than any other single party.

National Assembly The provincial parliament in Quebec.

nomination day Day 21 in an election countdown; the day a list with the names of the candidates is drawn up.

non-partisan Not influenced by and not supporting any one particular party.

Parliament The federal body that makes Canadian laws. It consists of the Queen's representative (the governor general), an appointed Senate and an elected House of Commons.

platform A candidate or party's list of plans and promises.

register of electors A list of the people eligible to vote in an election.

riding Another word for electoral district.

scrutineer An appointed party supporter who observes the proceedings at the polling station on election day.

Senate The Upper House of Parliament made up of those appointed by the prime minister.

Shadow Cabinet A group of official opposition party spokespeople who "shadow" specific Cabinet ministers.

slogan An election cheer that sums up what the candidate or party is saying and helps whip up interest and excitement.

spoiled ballot A ballot that has been torn or marked incorrectly.

suffragette A woman who speaks out and battles for the right to vote.

Index